Golf Cartoon and Trivia Book

By

William Kociemba

&

Eric A. Kaufman

Illustrated By

Steve Sack

Cover design by Michelle Fournier

Interior design by Michelle Fournier

Interior photographs courtesy of C3 Entertainment, Inc.

Published by Gazelle, Inc.
40940 County Center Drive
Temecula, California 92590
www.golfinstuff.com

First edition
Printed in Hong Kong

ISBN 0- 9667876- 2- 5

L-R Curly, Moe and Larry

Thank You

Moe, Larry, Shemp, Curly, Joe and Curly-Joe
for leaving us with a legacy of laughter.

Dedication

This book is dedicated to all the "scratch" golfers
out there, especially those that scratch their
heads after every other shot!

Acknowledgments

We'd like to thank the following people for their time
and talents in making this book possible:

C3 Entertainment, Inc. for providing photographs
and informative tidbits for the trivia sections.

Steve Sack for his patience and professionalism.
Nobody captures an expression better than him!

Jon Bass of *Reprints*, Inc., the illustrator of the Country
Club logo.

The talented Michelle Fournier of *The Graphics Dept.*
for her exceptional work in laying out this book.

O'Brian Kaufman, editor-at-large, for his literary skills.

Gary Kociemba, our very special consultant and number
one catalyst from early on.

To our wonderful wives, Esther and Candi, for their
continuous support.

And to the rest of our family and friends whose
encouragement and insights made this project fun.

Table of Contents

Introduction

Over the past six decades, millions of people have enjoyed the Three Stooges style of humor. Millions of others are enjoying the immensely popular game of golf.

This book, which has been written for the "Golf'n Stooges" throughout the world, includes history and humor about these two very interesting topics.

For Three Stooges fans, there are five different trivia sections along with a nostalgic Three Stooges photo album. For golf enthusiasts, there's a unique section called "Match Play" that highlights some of golf's legendary players during the early Stooge era. Tying all the sections together are more than 60 humorous Three Stooges golf cartoons in full color.

Enjoy ☺

Bill & Eric

BAD SLICE
ON #8

"WITH ALL DA NUTS AROUND HERE YOU'D THINK HE'D LEAVE THE DANG BALL ALONE!"

STOOGES 3-D GOLF:

DAPPER, DANGEROUS, & DINGY!

THE DREAM TEAM
TALLYING UP
ANOTHER "POIFECTLY"
PLAYED HOLE

Stooge Notes

MOE
CURLY
LARRY

JOE
SHEMP
CURLY-JOE

(Trivial Stuff about the Stooges™)
Answers found on page 25

1. Which Stooge impersonated a girl in an all-girl diving act?

2. Which Stooge accidentally shot himself in the foot with a .22 rifle?

3. Which one of the Stooges had an obsession for dogs?

4. What was Moe Howard's real name?

5. What was Shemp Howard's real name?

6. In addition to Larry, which of the Stooges had curly hair as a child?

7. What musical instrument did Larry play and why?

8. Which Stooge drove a car only once in his entire lifetime?

9. Which Stooge had the most phobias?

10. How did Moe acquire his unique bowl-type haircut?

11. What was Larry Fine's real name?

12. Which Stooge trained to be a boxer?

13. Which of the Stooges was an accomplished ballroom dancer?

14. Which of the Stooges had the best singing voice?

15. Did Shemp play the role of the third Stooge before or after Curly?

16. Which Stooge enjoyed hosting parties for the rich and famous?

17. Which Stooge appeared in silent movies at the age of 12?

18. Which Stooge would say "woob woob woob?"

19. Which Stooge married four times and fathered two children from different marriages?

20. Did the Three Stooges ever appear in a film with Laurel & Hardy?

21. At the age of 11, which Stooge attended school for only 40 days out of a possible 103?

22. When asked if he was a man or mouse, which Stooge replied "Squeak, Squeak?"

23. On their first family picnic together, which Stooge tossed tomatoes at a nearby family gathering causing a considerable brawl?

24. Who was the only Stooge to come from a showbiz family?

25. After Curly's stroke and retirement from the team, which Stooge suggested that the remaining team members each give Curly $50 per week to help their ailing brother and friend?

26. When asked what six plus six was, which Stooge replied "Boxcars?"

27. At age two, which Stooge was doing some dance steps on his father's jewelry showcase when he lost his balance and fell backwards through the glass of the display box?

28. Which Stooge told an actress that a bunch of half-hearted slaps hurt more than one good one?

29. Which Stooge mistakenly ate dog food on the set?

30. One of the greatest comedy teams of all times was the Three Stooges. Which Stooge performed for over 60 years without missing a single performance?

Answers To Trivia Questions

1. Moe. He wore a one-piece bathing suit with paper falsies for breasts when he toured with the *Annette Kellerman's Diving Girls*. After each dive, he would have to stay under water until he pushed the paper falsies back into place. Moe did a 30-foot dive into a tank seven feet long, seven feet wide and seven feet deep.

2. Curly. Accidents can happen and soitenly happened in his career. (See *Occupational Hazards of Being a Stooge* section.)

3. Curly. In the early vaudeville days, he would buy a dog in nearly every city that the Stooges played. He would keep it with him for about a week and then ship it home to Los Angeles.

4. His given name was Harry Moses Horwitz. In school he was known as Moe, a name that would later become legendary in show business.

5. Samuel Horwitz. His Hebrew name was Schmool which was Anglicized to Samuel or Sam. When his mother would pronounce Sam in her broad European accent, it sounded like Shemp!

6. Moe. By the time Moe was six years old (1903), his curly hair was almost to his shoulders. Moe's mother always wanted a girl (all five of her children were boys), so Moe would please his mother by allowing her to curl his hair every morning before school. As a result, Moe was constantly teased in school for his "girly hair," and was engaged in fist fights on almost a daily basis until he was 11-years-old.

7. The violin. When he was a small child, he burned his arm with acid and required a major skin graft. He was given a violin to play as therapy to repair the damaged nerves in his arm. Larry became an accomplished violinist, and used this talent in his early vaudeville act and Stooge shorts.

8. Shemp. Moe and Shemp went in as partners on their first car, a Pope Hartford that cost $90 used and had no brake linings. As part of the deal, Moe was to give Shemp driving lessons. During the lesson, Shemp let go of the steering wheel to squeeze the bulb horn with both hands. Before the horn went off, the car went through a barber shop window and stopped when it hit a barber's chair. Fortunately, the shop was closed. From that day forward, Shemp never drove a car again. In films where Shemp was supposed to be driving a car, it was actually being pulled along by a stuntman.

9. Shemp. He had a fear of driving, flying, heights, water and dogs. In the movie *Hold That Lion*, Shemp had to do a scene with an old sickly lion. Shemp was so frightened, that technicians had to put a glass plate between Shemp and the lion.

10. After years of being teased and bullied about his 10-inch long curls, Moe took a pair of scissors and circled his head clipping off all of his curls. The result was a bowl-shaped haircut.

11. Louis Fineburg. He was born October 5, 1902 in Philadelphia, Pennsylvania. His screen personality was as laid back as his real life one. He loved to throw parties, and was also known for his tardiness. Several times during his career, Moe had to cover for him until he showed up.

12. Larry. He was a lightweight boxer, who earned money by fighting in over 40 bouts. Larry was a man who could deliver or receive a punch with the best of them.

13. Curly. He was a graceful dancer that frequented night clubs. Remember the Curly shuffle?

14. Curly. He had a beautiful tenor voice.

15. Shemp actually was a Stooge along with his brother Moe before Larry joined the act. During the vaudeville and early movie years with Ted Healy (the original act was Ted Healy and his Stooges), the Stooges were Moe, Larry and Shemp. After disputes with Ted Healy, Shemp decided to leave the act and pursue what became a successful acting career. After Curly's first stroke in 1946, Shemp rejoined the Stooges in his younger brother's place. Shemp remained with the team until his death in 1955.

16. Larry. It's rumored that he also enjoyed stashing silverware in his pockets when attending other Hollywood parties.

17. Moe. In 1909, at the Vitagraph Studios in Brooklyn, Moe asked if there were any actors who might want someone to run errands. Within an hour he was running some errands, but decided not to accept any tips. Later when asked by an insider why he refused his tips, Moe replied, "Because I'm looking for a job in films." Impressed, the insider introduced Moe to the studio director, who then offered him a part in a film.

18. Curly. He was born in 1903, and was the youngest of five boys in the family. When Curly was about four, Moe and Shemp started to instill in their brother the idea of becoming a comedian. The three of them would set up a production in the basement of a friend's home, and charged two cents for admission. Another of his classic catch-phrases was N'yuk, N'yuk, N'yuk.

19. Curly. His first marriage, while in his teens, was to a young girl whose name remains a mystery to this day. His mother, Jennie Horwitz, the matriarch of the family, was against the marriage, and before six months had gone by, had the marriage annulled.

20. Yes. The film entitled *Hollywood Party* (MGM 1934) featured the Stooges, Laurel & Hardy and other stars of the day.

21. Moe. Absent cards were constantly being mailed to his house. As soon as the mailman would put them in the box, Moe would take them out. Then he would forge a note that Moses was attending school in his grandmother's neighborhood.

22. Joe Besser. Joe once said, "I love working for kids; they are my best fans, my best audience and my best friends. My biggest thrill is having kids like me. As long as this happens, I've got it made." He made 16 shorts with the Stooges, but left in 1958 to care for his sick wife Ernie.

23. Shemp. A man from the assaulted family came back screaming and dragging Shemp by the ear. With tomatoes dripping off his face and clothes, he shook Shemp like a rag doll. Infuriated, Shemp's mother Jennie jumped up and hit the man with her sun umbrella and a free-for-all started. When it was over, Shemp's father was lying against a tree with a bloody nose, Moe had been hit by assorted china, brother Irving was crying in the grass and everybody's clean clothes were dirty. When the confusion died down, Shemp got the beating of his life in front of the stranger. The stranger, Mr. Mitchell, apologized for shaking Shemp. Jennie then apologized for hitting Mr. Mitchell. Mr. Mitchell eventually became a family friend and a business partner with Jennie.

24. Curly-Joe DeRita. His mother was a dancer and his father a stage technician. He was also the only Stooge who wasn't Jewish. He came from French-Canadian and English ancestry. Joe was a heavy man that could do a graceful shuffle. His delivery was smooth and he was great at ad-libs. When he cut his hair, he resembled Curly; a definite favorite of the Stooge fans.

25. Larry. He was an extrovert who would spend his money as fast as he got it. At times he would lend money to actors and friends in need, never asking to be reimbursed.

26. Curly. He wasn't a "brain-soygen" but was a phenomenal entertainer who drew laughs by the millions. Curly's real name was Jerome Lester Horwitz. Moe gave him the nickname Babe.

27. Larry. He enjoyed putting on shows for anyone who would watch. His propensity for being a Stooge showed even at this tender age.

28. Shemp. In the short *Brideless Groom* (1947), the actress then proceeded to belt Shemp so often and so hard that she knocked him through a door. Later the actress put her arms around him and tearfully apologized. Painfully, Shemp said, "It's all right, honey, I said you should cut loose and you did. You sure the hell did."

29. Larry. Columbia prop man Stan Dunn remembers Larry was always hungry. Dunn once set a dish of dog food out for a training dog. Larry came by and ate the whole thing. When Larry found out what he had eaten, he allegedly turned green and said, "That was great! What brand was it?" Dunn also remembers Moe breaking his nose when he missed his timing going through a revolving door. And, on another occasion, Curly breaking his toe when he delivered a swift kick at Larry and hit a table leg instead.

30. Moe. He was the team leader the other Stooges depended on. He booked the appearances, negotiated the contracts and later decided who would be on the team. Once when asked how long the Stooges would remain in show business, Moe replied "Forever is a long time, but with a little luck we just might make it."

THE ODDS ON FAVORITES

COMING THROUGH

PLAYING A "DREAM ROUND"
TO A STANDING OVATION at
ICE CAPS COUNTRY CLUB

In the early years of the Stooges, they were known as Ted Healy and his Stooges. Ted Healy was a big vaudeville and film star of the period, as well as a childhood friend of Moe's. After several breakups, precipitated by Ted Healy's unfair treatment of the Stooges, Moe managed to convince Ted to release the Stooges from their contract with him and MGM. Larry and Curly were concerned about their ability to go out on their own, but Moe knew that there was a place for them in films... the question was where?

TWO REELER TRIVIA

That's when they decided to call themselves The Three Stooges. On the day the Stooges left Ted Healy and the MGM studio lot, they agreed to meet later that afternoon to discuss their future plans. Moe was approached by an agent from Columbia before he even got to his car. He went down to Columbia and was given a contract to make a two-reel comedy. At the same time, an agent from Universal Studios approached Larry as he was leaving the studio, so Larry accompanied that agent to Universal to sign a contract. Later that day the Stooges discovered that they were under contract with two studios at the same time. Since the time stamped on the Columbia contract was earlier than the Universal contract, the Stooges belonged to Columbia. What began as a one-picture contract, went on to become 24 years of two-reel comedies (1934-1958).

Two-reelers, otherwise known as "shorts," each less than 20 minutes in length, were produced by the studio as "curtain raisers" to be shown before a feature film presentation. Studio management considered the shorts to be "throwaways," and they paid little attention to their production as long as they were completed on schedule.

Since each short had to be shot in less than a week, time was of the essence. At Columbia, most of them had to be filmed in three days. The Stooges, however, were usually allowed an extra day of shooting time, primarily because of the often elaborate sight gags involved. Although the market for two-reel comedies began to fade, the demand for the Stooge shorts were very high among theater owners. At times, Columbia forced theater owners to take one of their "B" pictures if they wanted a Stooge two-reeler.

More on Moe

Head Over Heels

When Moe was very young, he kept falling off beds, over chairs and off tables. He never cried, never broke any bones, never even had a black and blue mark. His parents and friends thought it was uncanny. Finally, after falling off a penny picture machine, his face became a bloody mess. Moe was taken to a doctor who proceeded to stitch his nose on crooked. Several days later, Moe's mother, Jennie, noticed the botched job and went wild. She phoned the doctor to voice her displeasure. The doctor rushed over, took the bandage off, cleaned Moe's nose and began putting a new bandage on when Jennie walked up

to the doctor and belted him over the head a couple of times with a broom, yelling, "You ruined my son's face. You ruined him. You gave him a crooked nose." She continued to swat him as he descended the stairs.

Neither Moe's family nor anyone else in the neighborhood ever saw the doctor again. It was later discovered that he was practicing medicine in some areas without a license. A new doctor was found to correct the botched job of the previous doctor. He informed Jennie that because of ruptured eye nerves, he would lose his eyesight. Moe was blind for 11 months. His sight returned to normal by age four.

The Class Clown

From kindergarten on, Moe was a hell-raiser. One of his worst offenses was dipping little spitballs into the inkwell and blowing them at different kids in the room. One time he put some red ink in his mouth, laid his head on his desk and let the blood-colored ink ooze out. He was convincing, for it really scared the teacher and students. Later the principal and Moe's parents were called in. According to Moe, he and the kids had a good time, but he ended up paying for it later.

Scissors and Shivers

Because of his long hair, Moe claimed that by age 11 he sported more black eyes and bloody noses than any youngster alive… anywhere. On an impulse, he cut his own hair at a friend's house. He both laughed and cried knowing he had destroyed one of his mother's few pleasures. Unable to present himself to his mother, he hid in a nearby barn until dark and later underneath his porch. Laying in the dirt and shivering, he could hear his mother sobbing and his father describing to the police his long black curls and mass of freckles. At about two in the morning, shaking with chills and saddened by the weeping of his mother, he lightly coughed, then coughed a little louder to tip off his family as to his whereabouts. Upon seeing his mother, tears welled up in his eyes, then tears welled up in hers. She said softly, "Thank God you did it, I didn't have the courage."

Rollin' with the Flow

Moe's grades in elementary school were always excellent. His memory was so good that he never needed to bring any homework home. On test days, Moe would finish long before the others. Bored at times, he would let out a war-whoop like a crazed wild man. Once, after being sent to the cloakroom for his antics, he asked his teacher if he could go to the lavatory. She yelled no! Well he really had to go bad, so he ended up relieving himself in a flower pot. The problem was, however, the flower pot had drainage holes in it. It wasn't long before the clear yellow liquid ran out the bottom, under the cloakroom door and into the classroom.

Hobbies and Headaches

Later in life Moe enjoyed gardening. He had a green thumb, but also the problem of gophers and humans stealing his produce. Once, after staying up all night to catch the culprits, a couple of neighborhood kids showed up at the scene of the crime. Moe started chasing one of them and managed to get hit in the head with a rock by the kid he was chasing.

During this same period, Moe also raised chickens. When the time came for processing the chickens, Moe slammed a cleaver on a chicken's neck, and threw the bird into a barrel. When he heard the bird flapping around, it made him sick. Turning to get away from the awful sound, he glanced down and saw the chicken's head. When it appeared that one of the eyes was winking at him, he quit cleaning on the spot. A hired hand finished cleaning the birds. It was several months before he could eat chicken again.

Pie in the Eye

In the 1970s, the nostalgic craze of the Three Stooges ignited at the college level. Moe, in his 70s, was asked to do a speaking appearance at State University of New York, in Buffalo. Although the appearance was broadcasted on closed-circuit TV to all parts of the campus, the 1600-seat auditorium was filled to capacity, with another 400 students in standing-room-only.

After viewing a couple of two-reeler comedies, Moe went on to answer questions from cards the students had written on. One of the cards read, "Would you do me the honor of throwing a pie at me?" When the student approached Moe with the pie, he examined it and realized the pie was considerably heavier than the ones they used in their films. Moe explained the problem, but the young man wouldn't be deterred. Moe then threw the pie and it exploded on impact, sending the student back a good five feet. After the throw, the student was all smiles, and thanked Moe for the honor. In Moe's autobiography, *Moe Howard & The 3 Stooges*, he states that never in his show business career, with or without the other Stooges, had he enjoyed a standing ovation more than that one.

Moe, a high school dropout, continued on the college circuit, and occasionally did some TV talk shows around the Los Angeles area. In 1974, as a guest of the Mike Douglas Show, a vicious pie fight broke out at the tail end of the show. Moe wound up having the last pie. With pie in hand, he walked off the stage and into the audience where his wife, Helen, had been sitting in the front row. With camera's rolling, Moe leaned forward to kiss her. Then backing up a few steps, he turned and slammed the pie into the face of Soupy Sales, who was the co-host for that week.

Several months later, Moe made his third appearance on the Mike Douglas Show and again a pie fight broke out. Once again Moe ended up with the last pie. With pie in hand he walked towards Helen in the audience. This time instead of getting an affectionate kiss, she leaned forward and got the pie smashed right in her face. Laughing on national television, she proceeded to kiss Moe anyway, smearing the pie ingredients from her face to his.

On his fourth Mike Douglas appearance, Mike asked Moe to bring Helen up on stage to sit with him. Moe walked over to her and extended his hand to help her up. As he bent over, she reached for a concealed cream pie and slammed it right into his face. It was the first pie she had ever thrown, and she threw a bulls-eye! According to Moe, it was one of the high points of their long life together.

PLAYING THE HIGH
Lie-STOOGE STYLE

STRiKiNG iT... RiCH

YARDAGE MARKER

 **WISE GUYS 429 YDS.**

 **BULL FROGS 402 YDS.**

 **FISH BAIT 377 YDS.**

 **TAD POLES 351 YDS.**

AT THREE STOOGES COUNTRY CLUB FAILED **CHIP SHOTS**...

...OFTEN LEAD TO WELL-EXECUTED **CHEAP SHOTS!**

HAVING
A COURSE
CONNiPTiON in
LiViNG COLOR

Stooge Era
Golf Questions and Trivia
for the Golf'n Stooge

Answers found on page 70

1. The Three Stooges were masters at drawing attention. Which famous golf pro was also adept at drawing attention by arriving at club houses in a limousine, dressed in a tux?
   - (A) Ben Hogan
   - (B) Walter Hagen
   - (C) Bobby Jones
   - (D) Sam Snead

2. In golf, if you got an albatross you?
   - (A) Hit the wrong ball for a two-stroke penalty
   - (B) Had an uncontrollable desire to fling a club
   - (C) Played three under par on one hole
   - (D) Played four over par on one hole

3. The Three Stooges were one-of-a-kind in slapstick comedy. Which golfing phenom was the only person to ever win golf's "Grand Slam?"
   - (A) Harry Vardon
   - (B) Walter Hagen
   - (C) Bobby Jones
   - (D) Gene Sarazen

4. Back in the early Stooge era, a 4-iron was called a _____ , and a 2-wood was called a _____ ?
   - (A) Jigger and Brassie
   - (B) Baffie and Mashie
   - (C) Niblich and Spoon
   - (D) Quad and Spanker

5. What did Ben Hogan do in both his first and last professional tournament?
   (A) Scored two eagles
   (B) Tripped and fell from an untied shoestring
   (C) Quit and left before the tournament was over
   (D) Got sick on the course

6. At the age of 74, this golfer lived on the same property homesteaded by his grandfather?
   (A) Bobby Jones
   (B) Sam Snead
   (C) Henry Picard
   (D) Gene Sarazen

7. One way to describe the Three Stooges is to say that they were "an accident waiting to happen." Which famous golfer was nearly killed in an accident that did happen when a bus collided with his car?
   (A) Ben Hogan
   (B) Harry Vardon
   (C) Gene Sarazen
   (D) Sam Snead

8. Moe was the fourth of five boys in his family. In terms of age, what is the oldest major golf tournament played in the United States today?
   (A) Masters Tournament
   (B) U.S. Open
   (C) PGA
   (D) British Open

9. The Three Stooges overcame many obstacles in their career. While serving in the British tank corps in World War I, this golfer was hit in the left shoulder with shrapnel and lost sight in one eye after a mustard gas attack. Impressively, he still went on to win three of four modern-day Grand Slam events?
   A Tommy Armour
   B Ralph Guldahl
   C Jimmy Demaret
   D Harry Vardon

10. Knucklehead, Featherbrain and Dimwit were names Moe frequently called his fellow Stooges. Which one of these famous golfers was nicknamed the "Squire?"
    A Walter Hagen
    B Bobby Jones
    C Gene Sarazen
    D Ben Hogan

11. Driving cars from tournament to tournament was no picnic for the touring pros during the '30s. What did Byron Nelson and wife Louise do to keep warm in their car?
    A Lit a small kerosene heater
    B Cut a hole in the floor board and connected a steel bar to the engine
    C Snacked on hot Mexican food
    D Heated bricks

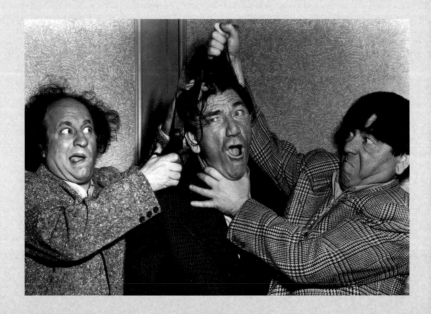

12. Which famous golfer caddied barefoot and nearly lost some of his toes from frost bite?

Ⓐ Byron Nelson
Ⓑ Walter Hagen
Ⓒ Ben Hogan
Ⓓ Sam Snead

13. Eye-popping, face-slapping and pie-throwing were antics that made the Stooges successful. "Calamity Jane" was an instrumental reason for which golfer's success?

Ⓐ Wyatt Earp
Ⓑ Ben Hogan
Ⓒ Bobby Jones
Ⓓ President Truman

14. Back in the '30s, a plus-two, plus-four or plus-six could have referred to your golf score or to?

Ⓐ A gambling wager
Ⓑ A point system used for birdies, pars, bogies, etc.
Ⓒ Clothing
Ⓓ The golf stance

15. The Three Stooges were famous for hitting each other. Since 1981, which famous three golfers hit the ceremonial tee shot to officially start the Masters?
    A) Byron Nelson
    B) Ben Hogan
    C) Bobby Jones
    D) Sam Snead
    E) Gene Sarazen

16. The official number of clubs allowed in your golf bag is?
    A) 12
    B) 13
    C) 14
    D) 15

17. At the young age of 17, Moe boarded a train to Jackson, Mississippi to audition for a part on the showboat *Sunflower*. By age 20, this golfer had already won both the U.S. Open and the PGA tournaments. He was also known to have made one of the most remarkable shots in golf history the famed – "shot heard 'round the world?"
    A) Walter Hagen
    B) Gene Sarazen
    C) Bobby Jones
    D) Ben Hogan

18. Some of the world's greatest golfers started out as caddies. Which two famous golfers tied in a nine-hole caddie tournament at Fort Worth's Glen Garden Country Club?
   (A) Sam Snead
   (B) Tommy Armour
   (C) Byron Nelson
   (D) Ben Hogan

19. The Stooges were in the business of making people laugh. How many business rounds of golf were played in 1997?
   (A) 850,000
   (B) 5 million
   (C) 10 million
   (D) 20 million

20. The Three Stooges were known to ad-lib and improvise their acts when needed. Which famous golfer also improvised by making his own clubs out of hickory and maple branches before turning pro?
   (A) Byron Nelson
   (B) Sam Snead
   (C) Walter Hagen
   (D) Ben Hogan

21. In regards to slapstick humor, the Three Stooges would be considered pros. Although this golfer never became a pro, he nonetheless received a ticker-tape parade in New York City?
    (A) Byron Nelson
    (B) Julius Boros
    (C) Bobby Jones
    (D) Jimmy Demaret

22. The Three Stooges were naturals in the comic arena. Which famous golfer, another true natural, reportedly never had a lesson?
    (A) Sam Snead
    (B) Bobby Jones
    (C) Gene Sarazen
    (D) Bob Hope

23. Golf balls were originally made of what material?
    (A) Wood
    (B) Feathers packed in a leather cover
    (C) Rubber
    (D) Cork

24. Hennie Bogan was a reason for Ben Hogan's success. Who or what was Hennie Bogan?
    (A) The name for his nerve-calming cigarettes
    (B) Nickname for his physical therapist after his crash
    (C) His favorite drink he had before each starting hole
    (D) His alter ego

25. The Three Stooges raised more than a few eyebrows in their career. During the 1989 U.S. Open, at Oak Hill Country Club, four golfers also raised eyebrows at the 167-yard 6th hole during one two-hour period when they did what?
    (A) Hit an ace or a 'hole-in-one'
    (B) Hit spectators – with two of them requiring medical attention
    (C) Hit balls that bounced off the pin
    (D) Hit a "porta potty" 40 yards right of the pin

26. For more than six decades the Three Stooges merchandise has been selling well. This golfer was the first American player to market golf equipment bearing his name?
   (A) Cary Middlecoff
   (B) Sam Snead
   (C) Arnold Palmer
   (D) Walter Hagen

27. Which famous golfer nearly died twice before the age of 12?
   (A) Sam Snead
   (B) Ben Hogan
   (C) Byron Nelson
   (D) Bobby Jones

28. This golfer was considered so cheap that when he had a nickel – he'd squeeze buffalo chips out of it?
   (A) Byron Nelson
   (B) Gene Sarazen
   (C) Walter Hagen
   (D) Sam Snead

29. Contrary to Stooge-Style play, this great golfer won the 1939 Western Open over the difficult Medinah #3 course near Chicago without leaving the fairway in 72 holes?
   (A) Sam Snead
   (B) Craig Wood
   (C) Byron Nelson
   (D) Just wishful thinking, it never happened

30. The Three Stooges were legendary comics, whose fame will last forever. Fame is also attained when a player wins a "Grand Slam" tournament. Golf's current "Grand Slam" includes the U.S. Open, the British Open, the Masters and the PGA. Of the following famous golfers, who can claim the most wins in the above mentioned tournaments? Who is second?
   (A) Walter Hagen
   (B) Ben Hogan
   (C) Sam Snead
   (D) Gene Sarazen
   (E) Bobby Jones
   (F) Byron Nelson
   (G) Arnold Palmer
   (H) Gary Player
   (I) Jack Nicklaus
   (J) Lee Trevino
   (K) Tom Watson

1. (B) Walter Hagen. During the Walter Hagen era, golf pros were low on the social ladder. Hagen was considered to be most responsible for raising the stature of professional golfers. He was a flamboyant individual who would arrive in a limousine and park next to the clubhouse he was barred from entering and then have his chauffeur serve lunch to him in the back of the car. Full complements of wine and silver settings were common. He played with kings and queens and, on one occasion, said to King Edward VIII, "Hey, Eddie, get the stick, will you?"

2. (C) It's a British term meaning you shot a double eagle or 3 under par on one hole. A Stooge-Style score of eight is sometimes referred to as a "snowman."

3. (C) Bobby Jones. In 1930, amateur Bobby Jones won the original "Grand Slam." This consisted of winning the U.S. Open, the U.S. Amateur, the British Open and the British Amateur all in the same year. After completing this "Grand Slam," Jones retired from tournament play at age 28. He later co-founded Augusta National Golf Course – home of the prestigious Masters Golf Tournament. (The current "Grand Slam" includes the U.S. Open, the British Open, the Masters and the PGA. No one has ever captured all four of these titles in a single year.)

4. (A) A 4-iron was a mashie iron or sometimes called a jigger, a 2-wood a brassie, a 3-wood a spoon, a 4-wood a cleek, a 5-wood a baffie; a 1-iron was a driving iron or cleek, a 2-iron a midiron, a 3-iron a mid-mashie, a 5-iron a mashie, a 6-iron a spated mashie, a 7-iron a mashie niblick, a 8-iron a pitching-niblick and a 9-iron a niblick.

5. (C) Hogan quit and left before the tournament was over. The first time, in the 1930 Texan Open, he quit because of mediocre play. Early in his last competitive round, in May 1971, in Houston, Hogan twisted his left knee – the same knee he injured in the car-bus accident 22 years earlier. Later, on the 11th tee, he swung and slipped so badly he almost fell. He had his caddie pick up the ball and said, "So long" to his playing partners, Dick Lutz and Charles Coody. He then rode back to the clubhouse in a cart with his arms crossed and his eyes down. His playing career was over.

STOOGE AGE

AUGUST 1952   **25¢**   **VOLUME 27 No. 6⁷/₈**

6. (B) Sam Snead. The old saying, "You can take the boy out of the country, but you can't take the country out of the boy!" certainly applied to him. Snead claimed that in his youth, the greatest danger living in the Virginia hills was not wildcats or bears, but accidentally stumbling onto a hidden still during the moonshine days. Snead said he narrowly missed taking a load of buckshot more than once. He kept that country boy feeling alive by wearing a "breathable" straw hat on the course, which resembled the hat his father used while working on the farm. At 74, Snead still lived in Hot Springs, Virginia, and was still a teaching pro there.

7. (A) Ben Hogan. The head-on collision nearly blinded him in his left eye, crushed his left leg, fractured his left collar bone, left ankle, pelvis and a rib. Doctors feared he might not walk again, much less play golf. Sixteen months after the accident, with his legs wrapped in bandages, he won the 1950 U.S. Open.

8. (B) The U.S. Open. It was played at St. Andrew's Golf Course in Yonkers, New York in 1894. The first officially sanctioned U.S. open was played in 1895. The PGA began in 1916 and the Masters in 1934. If you answered the British Open, you probably think it was played in Boston and the golfers drank tea instead of whiskey in the clubhouse. The oldest major golf tournament, the British Open, was first held in Scotland in 1860.

9. (A) Tommy Armour. The Silver Scot won the U.S. Open in '27, the PGA in '30 and the British Open in '31. The Masters Tournament began in 1934. According to Byron Nelson, Armour could really tell stories, and had the greatest gift of gab of anyone he knew. Armour was also an excellent golf instructor who occasionally drank a breakfast of scotch and bromo-selzer in separate glasses.

10. (C) Gene Sarazen. His sideline as an apple grower coupled with his habit of dressing to a tee (knickers were de rigueur on the links) earned Sarazen the nickname the "Squire."

11. (D) Heated bricks. Back then cars didn't have heaters to cut the chill of winter travel. Louise heated bricks in an oven, wrapped them in paper, and put them on the floor of their car. There were no radios, defrosters or air conditioners. The roads were rough, the tires were noisy and good for only 10-15,000 miles. Tires were sometimes deflated to prevent blowouts on hot days. Spark plugs usually failed after about 8,000 miles. To prolong battery life, drivers sometimes switched off their lights and drove by the light of the moon. Distance between tournaments could be substantial, while the purses were far from it.

12. (D) Sam Snead. As a teenager he liked to caddie barefoot. Once, while caddying in the snow, he nearly lost some toes. Years later, while playing in France, Snead played a match with three other ex-caddies. Before the match was over, three ex-kings – the Duke of Windsor, a Maharaja and King Leopold of Belgium followed them. This may have been the only time in golf history where three ex-kings followed four ex-caddies. Only in golf! (Byron Nelson, Ben Hogan, Harry Vardon, Gene Sarazen and Lee Trevino were other legends who started golf careers as caddies).

13. (C) "Calamity Jane" was Bobby Jones' famous putter. Bobby Jones was the greatest amateur and perhaps the greatest golfer of all time. In eight years he won 13 of the 27 major tournaments he entered. In 1958, he became the first American since Benjamin Franklin (1759) to receive the Freedom of the Burgh of St. Andrews, Fife, Scotland, home of the world's premier golf club. Jones never lost his amateur status, and stopped playing golf in 1949, because of a crippling illness.

14. (C) Clothing. Plus-two's, four's or six's referred to how many inches below the knee your knickers ended.

15. (A D, & E) Byron Nelson, Sam Snead and Gene Sarazen. In the 1999 Masters, 97-year-old Gene Sarazen hit his drive 140 yards down the left side of the fairway.

16. (C) 14. Golf'n Stooges, however, are also allowed a crochet mallet to be used only in times of great distress. N'Yuk N'Yuk N'Yuk.

17. (B) Gene Sarazen. In the last round in the 1935 Masters Golf Tournament, he holed a 235-yarder with a 4-wood on the 15th for a double-eagle two, the rarest shot in golf. The next day, in a two-man playoff, he went on to beat Craig Wood.

18. (C & D) Byron Nelson and Ben Hogan. Nelson won a 9-hole playoff by one stroke. They had many similarities – they grew up in the same city, had the same family doctor, never had kids, went by their middle names, dominated in the same era and were inducted into two major Halls of Fame in the same year. They also occasionally followed each other in cars going from tournament to tournament.

19. (D) It's estimated that more than 20 million business rounds were played in 1997. This gives new meaning to the words "course management."

STOOGE AGE

MAY 1925   **5¢**   **VOLUME 1 No. 3⁷/₈**

20. (B) Sam Snead. He won more tournaments than any other golfer. From 1936-1965, Snead won a record 81 tournaments sanctioned by the Professional Golfer's Association, and has claimed a total of 165 tournament victories. He became known as "Slammin' Sammy" for his powerful drives and naturally smooth swing.

21. (C) Bobby Jones. After winning the 1930 British Open, he was honored in a ticker-tape parade in New York. In 1930, at the peak of his career, he retired from tournament play and went on to practice law. The general public called him Bobby, his closest friends, however, called him Bob. Ben Hogan also received a ticker-tape parade down Broadway.

22. (A) Sam Snead. He and Byron Nelson are credited for developing the modern golf swing. He was also the oldest player to win a PGA event. At age 52 he won the 1965 Greater Greensboro Open by five strokes.

23. (A) Wood. Initially golf was played with crude wooden balls. For several centuries, up until the 1850s, golf was played with the feathery ball. This consisted of packing boiled-down goose and chicken feathers into an untanned bull's hide. A skilled Scottish ball maker could produce only three to four "featheries" a day, each costing four times the price of a club. Back then golf was indeed a game for the wealthy.

24. (D) His alter ego. Hennie Bogan was an imaginary person who pushed Hogan to excel. When asked in a 1991 ESPN interview: "The Ben Hogan work ethnic… who instilled that in you?" Hogan unabashedly replied: "Hennie Bogan." Hogan was the epitome of hard work in golf. At times, he practiced so long that his hands bled.

25. (A) Hit aces. The four players, Doug Weaver, Jerry Pate, Nick Price and Mark Wiebe all used 7-irons to make their hole-in-one. The aces occurred early in the morning and were not caught on film.

26. (D) Walter Hagen. He became the first golfer to earn more than $1 million in tournaments and exhibitions. Hagen appeared in more than 2,500 exhibitions throughout the world. In his autobiography *The Walter Hagen Story,* he said, "I never wanted to be a millionaire, I just wanted to live like one."

27. (C) Byron Nelson. The first time he nearly died was at birth. His mother experienced a very difficult delivery. The doctor thought he wouldn't survive, and centered his attention on his mother. Nelson was told he weighed 12 pounds, 8 ounces at birth.

The second near-death situation occurred when he contracted typhoid fever. At age 11, Nelson and some neighborhood kids were infected with rabies from a neighbor's dog. The kids were taken to Austin, Texas to receive one rabies inoculation a day for 21 straight days. Around the 15th day, Nelson started feeling really sick, probably from the water he drank. After the 21 days of treatment, the kids were taken back to Fort Worth. When Nelson's mother went to pick him up, she immediately sensed something was wrong and figured he had typhoid fever because of the way he smelled. Her husband had come down with typhoid fever shortly after they were married. A doctor confirmed her suspicion. Nelson was about 5 feet 8 tall at the time and weighed 124 pounds. Within a few weeks, his weight had dropped to 65 pounds, and the doctors had pretty much given up on him. But a female chiropractor, who was a member of Nelson's church, thought she could cure him. After about 10 days of treatment, he started feeling better and eventually recovered.

Surviving these two near-death experiences, along with the many friendships that developed in his life, are just two of the main reasons Nelson said he always felt that he was a blessed man.

28. (D) Sam Snead. Times were tough for him and his five brothers and sisters while farming in the mountains of Virginia. As a kid, he would catch trout with his hands. According to Snead, the trout would hide under rocks and logs. All he had to do was to reach under carefully and feel for one. With trout, if you move slow and gentle, you could rub their bellies. They liked it. Then you could just grab them. One day he grabbed what he thought was a trout, although it felt a little different. What he pulled out was a poisonous water moccasin. Luckily, he had a good hold on the snake and escaped unharmed.

29. (C) Byron Nelson. He played the 72-hole tournament without leaving the fairway. (Author's note: I personally know a golfer who played 72 holes without ever being in the fairway). ☺

30. (I) Jack Nicklaus – first place with 18 major championships.
(A) Walter Hagen – second place with 11 major championships.

Current
GRAND SLAM
Tournaments

	U.S. Open	British Open	Masters Tournament	PGA	Total Wins	Comments
Tournament Origin	1895	1860	1934	1916		
Harry Vardon 1870-1937	1	6	NP	NP	7	*1
Walter Hagen 1892-1969	2	4	0	5	11	*2
Bobby Jones 1902-1971	4	3	NP	NP	7	*3
Gene Sarazen 1902-1999	2	1	1	3	7	*4
Ben Hogan 1912-1997	4	**1	2	2	9	*5
Sam Snead 1912-	0	**1	3	3	7	*6
Byron Nelson 1912-	1	0	2	2	5	*7
Arnold Palmer 1929-	1	2	4	0	7	*8
Gary Player 1935-	1	3	3	2	9	*9
Lee Trevino 1939-	2	2	0	2	6	*10
Jack Nicklaus 1940-	4	3	6	5	18	*11
Tom Watson 1949-	1	5	2	0	8	*12
Joe Howard 1897-1975	0	0	0	0		*13

Totals do not include Senior Tour or major amateur tournament wins.
*Comments on the following pages **Competed only once   NP – never participated.

*1 - Englishman Harry Vardon helped popularize golf in the United States. American golfers like Bobby Jones admired the way he played. He made two extended tours of the U.S. in 1900 and 1913. Competing three times in the U.S. open, he won in 1900, lost in a playoff in 1913 and was again runner-up in 1920, while playing at age 50. Vardon is said to have been self-taught, and to have never had a lesson. He was probably the first professional golfer to commercially use his name on balls and clubs. In 1898, he had a contract with Spalding. The Vardon Trophy is awarded to the professional golfer with the lowest stroke average each year.

*2 - Walter Hagen was known to occasionally give his cash winnings to his caddie. Hagen used to say if he didn't hit more than seven bad shots in a round he figured he played a hell of a round. He also said, "You must adjust to conditions. If you fuss about every little thing that bothers you, you're not going to play. And if you don't play, you'll wind up turning into a piece of furniture in the clubhouse."

*3 - Bobby Jones also won the U.S. Amateur five times and the British Amateur once. These tournaments were part of golf's original "Grand Slam." Jones was phenomenal on British soil. He won three out of four British Opens, and one out of four British Amateurs, for a .500 winning average. In 24 major championships played in the States, he was successful nine times – a .375 winning average. In 1930, Jones played an exhibition match with British amateur Joyce Wethered. They played the Old Course at St. Andrews from the championship tees. Jones recalls: "Miss Wethered... did not miss a shot; she did not even half miss one shot; and when finished I could not help saying that I had never played golf with anyone, man or woman, amateur or professional, who made me feel so utterly outclassed. I have no hesitancy in saying that she is the finest golfer I have ever seen." Wethered shot a 75.

*4 - Gene Sarazen was the first of only four golfers to win all four tournaments in today's "Grand Slam." The other three were Ben Hogan, Gary Player and Jack Nicklaus. Sarazen won 38 PGA Tour titles, and is credited with developing the sand wedge. He was born Eugenio Saraceni, but changed his name because he thought it sounded too much like a violin player. He stopped playing golf in 1973, but went out in fashion with a hole-in-one at the Postage Stamp hole at Royal Troon. In 1923, he signed a contract with Wilson

Sporting Goods, which has been renewed every two years since. Just before his 97th birthday, he re-signed for his 76th and 77th years with the company. Sarazen nearly died during a flu epidemic in 1918.

5 - Ben Hogan, through hours of practice, was known for his relentless determination to perfect his swing. He won eight of the 11 majors he entered during one five-year stretch. He was 5 feet 8 tall and was one of the lightest champions, weighing only 135 pounds. He went on to win more than 60 tournaments in his career. In 1953, he nearly captured the "Grand Slam" title – failing only to win the PGA Tournament.

Hogan's mindset from early on was one of perfection. Once, after shooting a 64, including 10 birdies at Oak Hill Golf Club, he went back to the practice area and hit until dark. When golf pro Jimmy Demaret stopped and asked him what he was trying to prove, Hogan responded, "Jimmy, there's no reason in the world why a man can't birdie every hole." He's also quoted as saying, "If you can't hold a three-stroke lead through six holes, you ought to be someplace else."

Hogan could also deadpan on occasion. When asked what's the secret to his great ball-striking, Hogan replied, "Not telling." And when asked what was needed to win the U.S. Open, Hogan shot back, "Shoot the lowest score." Hogan offered this insight: "You can hit your shots great and still shoot 80 every day because of poor management. The shots are 30 percent of the game, judgment is 70 percent."

Hogan used to check the quality of his balls by putting them in a bathtub filled with water and Epsom salts. He marked a ball and spun it. If one side of a ball consistently floated downward, he knew the rubber bands inside had been wound unevenly. Only perfectly wound balls made it into his bag.

At the '53 Masters, Hogan stunned the crowd with a 14-under-par 274, beating the tournament record by five strokes. "The greatest four scoring rounds ever," Gene Sarazen told the press. "That's as good as I can play," Hogan said. "Practice means as much as playing itself. A tournament is an anti-climax to preparation, the way I see it."

Australian pro Peter Thompson had this to say about Hogan: "He could go a whole tournament, that's four rounds, without mishitting once. I've seen him do it. He was quite a contrast with Arnold

Palmer, who could hardly go three holes without hitting one sideways... The precision of Hogan's striking was incredible. I don't believe anybody today has approached that, not even Nicklaus."

One of the lowest points in Hogan's career happened back in 1938. Having just $86 left out of a budgeted $1,400, Ben and his wife Valerie were concerned. They agreed beforehand that they would spend all $1,400 if they had to. So they decided to drive to the next tournament in Oakland. Getting ready to leave the hotel for the first round of the tournament, Hogan found his car resting on cinder blocks. Thieves not only stole the tires, but the jack too. Byron Nelson eventually gave him a lift to the tournament.

One of his highest points happened in 1953. He won the U.S. Open, the Masters and had just returned from Scotland after winning the British Open. He landed in New York and received a hero's welcome – a ticker-tape parade down Broadway. Little did anyone know at the time that Ben Hogan had just won his last major tournament.

*6 - Sam Snead won the British Open, the Masters and the PGA, but never the U.S. Open. In 1939, he came close, but lost when he took an eight on the final hole. Uninformed of how the field was doing in front of him, Snead felt he had to be aggressive to win. If they had scoreboards back in '39 like they do today, he would have realized that he only needed bogies on the 17th and 18th holes to win. Snead's playing partner was told on the 17th hole how the other players did. For some reason, no one offered this information to him. Snead placed second in the U.S. Open four times.

Like Byron Nelson, Snead also carded a 59. He had 29 aces, routinely hit drives in excess of 300 yards, won golf championships in over six decades and had a contract with Wilson that lasted more than 50 years. Not bad for a country boy who cut hickory and maple branches for clubs, and who practiced maneuvering his balls around the chicken pens and outhouse, and on one occasion, right through a church window.

Australian pro Peter Thompson once said: "Like classic plays and symphonies, Sam Snead doesn't just belong to a generation, his mark will be left on golf into eternity."

Ben Hogan, Sam Snead and Byron Nelson were all born within seven months of each other in 1912. In all the tournaments they played in together, they only finished 1-2-3 once, in the 1946 Houston Open.

STOOGE AGE

OCTOBER 1939   10¢   VOLUME 14 No. 4⁷/₈

*7 - Byron Nelson set records in 1945 when he won 11 tournaments in succession, and 18 of 34 tournaments that year. During that stretch he also placed second seven times. Nelson had 61 tournament victories, and still holds the record for the lowest scoring average in a year, 68.3, in 1945. He retired, at 34, after a six-victory season in 1946.

In Byron Nelson's autobiography, *How I Played The Game*, he states that one of his proudest moments was when Bobby Jones asked him to play with the leader in the final round of the Masters. Before 1946, Bobby Jones had always played the first round of the Masters with the defending champ, and the last round with the tournament leader. When Jones became too ill to play, he asked Nelson to take his place. Nelson played the final round with the leader from 1946 until 1955. In 1956 Ken Venturi was the leader. The committee then decided that since Nelson and Venturi had worked so closely together, it would be unfair to the rest of the field to let them play together. After that it was decided to pair up the leader with whoever was closest for the final round.

Another of Nelson's most satisfying moments happened when he got involved with a group of men called the Salesmanship Club of Dallas. This was an organization that sponsored a highly successful, year-round outdoor camp for troubled boys, and later girls. In 1967 the Salesmanship Club was sponsoring the Dallas Open. They met with Nelson, who was going to be doing some commentary, and told him that ticket sales were very slow. At that point, Arnold Palmer had not entered the tournament and asked Nelson if he'd be willing to call him. Nelson agreed, and Arnold Palmer agreed to play. Two days after it was announced that Arnold Palmer would play, they sold 5,000 tickets. The following year the Salesmanship Club felt their tournament would be enhanced if they had a well known golfer connected to it. They asked Nelson for his permission to rename the Dallas Open the "Byron Nelson Golf Classic." Nelson agreed and said "It's become the best thing that ever happened to me in golf, better than winning the Masters, the U.S. Open or 11 in a row. Because it helps people." What pleased Nelson the most, was that all the profits from the tournament went to charity.

On Nelson's 80th birthday, in February, 1992, a nine-foot bronze sculpture of Nelson was unveiled in his honor and placed next to the "Byron Nelson Golf Classic" Wall of Champions.

8 - Arnold Palmer, known for his gambling style of playing, led many to believe that he was the man who single-handedly made golf a major sport. Winning more than 90 tournaments (60 on the PGA Tour) his career spanned a remarkable six decades. Palmer won at least one event in each of 17 consecutive years, a record tied only by Jack Nicklaus.

9 - When Gary Player won the Masters in 1978, the span of his major championship victories covered three decades, longer than any previous golfer. Player has won more than 140 tournaments around the world, including 21 on the PGA Tour.

10-When asked if he ever went to college, Lee Trevino replied, "Sure I went to college. I delivered Christmas trees to SMU." The "Super Mex" was known for his quick wit and great golfing skills. Trevino won 27 times on the PGA tour.

11-When Jack Nicklaus won his sixth Masters title in 1986, he became both the oldest and youngest player to win this most prestigious event. In 1997, Tiger Woods became the youngest winner of the Masters. Nicklaus has won 70 PGA Tour events around the world. In 1988 he was named, "Golfer Of The Century."

12-Tom Watson won 34 times on the PGA tour. Once, after witnessing a bad shot by Bob Hope, Watson said, "That one must have been hit by your brother, No Hope."

*13-Although Moe never played professional golf, he had some of the characteristics of the great players – a lot of nerve, great eye-hand coordination and fierce determination.

When Moe was 17, he saw an ad in a magazine that interested him. The ad was from Captain Billy Bryant. He was looking for a young man of average height to do some acting on his showboat, the *Sunflower*. He also requested a photo from all the applicants. Being only 5 feet 4 tall and weighing just 120 pounds, Moe felt his chances of getting an interview would improve if he sent a picture of his averaged-size, photogenic neighbor instead. The ploy worked and Moe even received, as requested, an advanced train fare from New York to Jackson, Mississippi. When Moe and Captain Bryant first met, he became furious knowing Moe had pulled a bit of a sham Moe broke in pleading, "You wouldn't gain a thing if you put me in jail. Putting me to work – even on menial jobs – would benefit you in the long run. And, you'd also know that you were instrumental in helping me towards my goal."

After some serious thought the Captain hesitantly responded, "Boy, you've got yourself a job... doing something or the other." Thanking him profusely, Moe said, "You know, Captain Bryant, I'm going to be an actor – a very good one!" Captain Bryant finally smiled and said, "With your ungodly nerve, I believe you can be anything."

Moe soon received his first professional acting job from Captain Bryant. He stayed two seasons and was extremely pleased with the outcome.

The Occupational Hazards of being a Stooge™

The Stooges rarely used stunt doubles and were very adept at taking falls. However, the job description for being a Stooge meant that you were inevitably in for some bumps and bruises. Here is a list of some trivial and not so trivial injuries suffered by the boys during their careers as Stooges:

In their first short with Columbia, *Woman Haters* (1934), Larry broke his finger while tumbling out of a sleeping berth during a scene in a Pullman car.

In their second film, *Punch Drunks* (1934), Curly played a prize fighter who would go crazy when Larry played *Pop Goes the Weasel* on his violin. Curly suffered a bloody nose and a cut lip while playing a scene in the ring with a professional boxer.

In the film *Men In Black* (1934), the Stooges were cut by flying glass when they slammed shut a glass door in one of the hospital scenes.

For their first football film, *Three Little Pigskins* (1934), the football scenes were shot with football players from Loyola University. According to Moe, "They knew how to tackle and they tackled hard." During the touchdown run scene, Moe, Larry and Curly were supposed to stop for news photographers on the sideline where they are pounced on by the entire Loyola football team. When the Stooges reviewed this scene they saw trouble with an entire team of 200-pounders pouncing on top of them. The Stooges informed the director that they wanted stunt doubles to do this scene. They never used stunt doubles before, but they knew that they needed them now. The director, Raymond McCarey, said, "Listen, fellows, you know how to take falls. You've done enough of them. It will take hours to find doubles for you. Besides, we can't afford them. Don't worry, you won't get hurt." The Stooges still refused to do the scene and within an hour stunt doubles were on the field, ready for the scene. During the scene, all of the players, including the doubles, landed in a heap on top of the newsmen. As the heap unraveled, two of the stunt doubles had broken legs, all four newsmen had either broken arms or legs and all of them wound up in the hospital except for Curly's stunt double. Apparently, he was padded all over to resemble Curly and the padding broke the blows.

During a scene in *Ants in the Pantry* (1936), the Stooges played exterminators. Since they were having trouble selling their services, their boss said, "If they don't have bugs, then give them some." So the Stooges went from house to house throwing mice on the floor and ants in the pantry. In one scene, Moe hadn't noticed that a container of red ants had broken in his pocket and they were crawling down his back, in his hair and into his pants. Throughout the scene, Moe was scratching, squirming and slapping himself on the neck and the seat of his pants. The elated director screamed, "Great Moe. Keep up that squirming."

In the film *Hoi Polloi* (1935), a scene called for the leading lady, Grace Goodall, to laugh loudly with her mouth wide open while Moe hit her in the face with a cream puff. Moe, who was a perfect shot due to his childhood experience with pea shooters and spitballs, hit Grace squarely in the mouth with the cream puff. It lodged so deeply down her throat, that some of the cream had gone down her windpipe, forcing her to gasp for breath. There were some moments of concern, but they finally brought her around.

More than 150 pies were thrown during the 16-minute comedy *Slippery Silks* (1936). An emergency arose when they ran out of pies. The property man came onto the set and swept up all of the whipped cream he could collect from the floor to make a new batch of pies. Inside the dirty whipped cream were dust, nails and splinters. Fortunately, nobody was injured when they were hit in the face with pies full of nails. The show must go on!

Although Moe played the toughest character of the Stooges and always seemed to dish out more of the punishment than he received, he was hurt more often than Larry or Curly. Moe landed in the hospital after a scene in *Beer and Pretzels* (1933). Moe was standing on a table that Curly was cutting with a circular saw. When the table broke, Moe was suppose to break his fall but the side of his body hit the upright legs of the table. He spoke the remainder of his lines and then passed out. Later, he learned that he had three broken ribs.

In a film where the boys were playing women wearing high-heeled shoes, Moe was skipping and one heel turned under him. In order to avoid ruining the shot, Moe slid to the side and dove into another room where he hit his head on the leg of a bed that knocked him out cold. The next day he was on crutches with a broken ankle.

Curly cut his scalp one day during a stunt where he was supposed to be dropped down an elevator shaft. The shaft was a hole large enough for Curly to disappear off camera. The floor of the hole was padded with a mattress, but the property guys neglected to cover a nearby two-by-four. When Curly was pushed into the hole, he cut his head on the two-by-four. The studio doctor clipped the hair around the wound, cleaned it and then proceeded to glue fresh hair onto the bald spot. Curly then continued on with the scene.

Larry had his share of accidents as well. He was hit in the eye with plaster, had a tooth knocked out and was even stabbed in the forehead with a quill pen.

Yes, the occupation of being a

STOOGE™

was a hazardous one!

BEST SHOT OF THE DAY

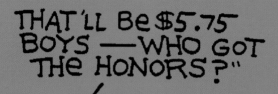

A.A.M.
AMALGAMATED ASSOCIATION
OF MORONS LOCAL 6 7/8

Entrance Exam
Answers found on page 123

The Amalgamated Association of Morons Local 6 7/8 requires all candidates to take this entrance exam to determine eligibility in joining this elite organization. The test will evaluate your background on hodgepodge, medical science, history, music appreciation, foreign language and "Stooge English." Please answer the following questions with a No. 3 1/2 pencil. Cheating on this exam will result in a poke in the eyes.

Good luck!

1. What is the Amalgamated Association of Morons Local 6 7/8?

   Ⓐ A labor union that provides protection for pie throwing.

   Ⓑ A men's only club located in the Country of Moronica where Curly does the Curly shuffle in drag.

   Ⓒ A union representing the "fruitcake" industry.

   Ⓓ The offshore corporation that the Stooges used to shelter money from the I.R.S.

   Ⓔ The national affiliate of the Mensa Organization.

2. In 1922, Ted Healy and Moe were in an act together. Ted Healy was earning $3,500 per week. What was Moe earning?

(A) $1,000
(B) Approximately $5,000
(C) $100
(D) Two cents
(E) The same

3. What was the occupation of Curly's mother, Jennie?

(A) Actress
(B) Teacher
(C) Successful real estate agent
(D) Mental health evaluator
(E) Social worker

4. Three of these four characters were brothers. Who was not?

(A) Moe
(B) Curly
(C) Larry
(D) Shemp

5. How many shorts and feature films did the Stooges make after they went out on their own and became the Three Stooges?

(A) 190 shorts, 6 features.
(B) 71 shorts, 12 features.
(C) 241 shorts, 3 features.
(D) Just a pair of shorts that were featured in the first laundry detergent commercial.

6. Under the name The Three Stooges, their films were made during what time period?

(A) 1910-1941
(B) 1919-1955
(C) 1934-1965
(D) Made in China a heck of a long time ago.

7. If Moe was considered the first Stooge and Larry the second, how many different third Stooges were there?
   (A) two
   (B) three
   (C) four
   (D) five

8. Back in 1962, the leading attraction at local movie theaters were?
   (A) Five-cent Milk Duds.
   (B) Ten-cent bottled pop.
   (C) Getting the darker back row seats with your current flame.
   (D) The Three Stooges shorts.

9. The oldest of the Three Stooges brothers was?
   (A) Moe
   (B) Curly
   (C) Larry
   (D) Shemp

Medical

10. What names did the Stooges use when they portrayed doctors in their films?

   Ⓐ Dr. Howard, Dr. Fine, Dr. Howard
   Ⓑ Dr. Hart, Dr. Burns and Dr. Belcher
   Ⓒ Dr. Ziller, Dr. Zeller and Dr. Zoller
   Ⓓ Dr. D. Lerious, Dr. Graves and Dr. I. Yankum
   Ⓔ A, B & C

History

11. In the civil war spoof, *Uncivil Warriors*, Larry played Lieutenant Duck and Moe played Captain Dodge. What was the name of the character that Curly played in this film?

   Ⓐ General Weave
   Ⓑ Major Run
   Ⓒ Corporal Dig.
   Ⓓ Major Hyde
   Ⓔ Private Flee

Music Appreciation

12. What sound effect was used for the famous Three Stooges eye poke?

   Ⓐ An accordion
   Ⓑ Voice-over sounds from Larry
   Ⓒ Whistling by famous Stooge film director Jules White
   Ⓓ A slide whistle
   Ⓔ The plucking of ukulele strings

Foreign Language

13. These lines were spoken in various Stooge films. *"Ver G'harget"*; *"123 Mashugana Avenue"*; *"Huck mir nisht a chynick, and I don't mean efsher!"* What foreign language, or fictional foreign language is this and what are the translations?

(A) Yiddish. "Drop dead"; "123 Crazy Avenue"; "Don't bother me, get off my back and I don't mean maybe!"

(B) Moronica. "Knucklehead"; "123 Mashugana Avenue" (no translation); "Hey bunionhead, taste this pie and I don't mean eat it!"

(C) German. "Don't look now"; "123 Kraut Avenue" "Hey puddin' head, take this, and I don't mean that!"

(D) Hebrew. "Bunion brain"; "123 Nuts Avenue"; "Hey Gorilla, back into the cage and I don't mean monkey!"

(E) None of the above. The Stooges made up words in some films as part of the gags.

Stooge English

Instructions: In the following section, match the phrases to the
Stooge whom so eloquently speaked 'em.

14. "I'm trying to think, but nothing happens."
    (A) Moe   (B) Curly   (C) Larry   (D) Shemp

15. "Wake up and go to sleep."
    (A) Moe   (B) Curly   (C) Larry   (D) Shemp

16. "You were delivered by a buzzard."
    (A) Moe   (B) Curly   (C) Larry   (D) Shemp

17. "You told me to drop what I was doing, so I did."
    (A) Moe   (B) Curly   (C) Larry   (D) Shemp

18. "You're a very intelligent imbecile."
    (A) Moe   (B) Curly   (C) Larry   (D) Shemp

19. "I'm going to get myself a cheap lawyer."
    (A) Moe   (B) Curly   (C) Larry   (D) Shemp

20. "Are you married or happy?"
    (A) Moe   (B) Curly   (C) Larry   (D) Shemp

21. Moe and Shemp did all of the following together except?
  (A) Purchased their first car
  (B) Grew beards on only one side of their face
  (C) Married sisters
  (D) Once tried to talk some gals into skinny-dipping

22. When Moe was 11-years-old he frequently attended the theater. How did he pay for his tickets?
  (A) Sold frogs to a local saloon
  (B) Had a fruit stand on 12th and A Street
  (C) Washed dishes after wedding receptions
  (D) Never paid! He would sneak through a window in the basement

23. In the short, *A Pain In the Pullman*, the Stooges ended up in a room with a table of delicacies. How did Curly open up his crab shell?
  (A) He broke a bottle over it
  (B) He used a sledge hammer
  (C) He tapped danced on it
  (D) He had Moe do it because he couldn't get it open

24. Which actress played Daisy Simms in the Three Stooges short –
Three Little Pigskins?
   (A) Rita Hayworth
   (B) Ginger Rogers
   (C) Phylliss Diller
   (D) Lucille Ball

25. The Stooges played golf in which film?
   (A) *Sticks and the Stones*
   (B) *Three Little Beers*
   (C) *Putt, Putt, Poof*
   (D) *Birdie Brains*
   (E) *Fore Practice Makes Poifect*

26. The Stooges did all of the following except?
   (A) Innumerous benefits for charitable organizations
   (B) Once informed a belligerent customer that if he kept it up,
       he might go from 32 teeth to zero
   (C) Picked on the rich and powerful
   (D) They did all of the above

27. In 1958, when the Stooges worked a club in Bakersfield, they earned
$2,500 for the week. Just a short time later the Stooges were offered
as much as $25,000 a day to dedicate a shopping mall in New York.
What happened?
(A) They started showing Three Stooges shorts on television
(B) Veteran vaudeville star Curly-Joe DeRita joined the act
(C) They started doing feature films
(D) They hired Moe Manly, New York's best talent agent

28. In a fit of rage, Shemp once hit Veronica right in the eye.
Who was Veronica?
(A) Greta Garbo's sister
(B) A chicken
(C) Make-up girl that sabotaged his tuna fish sandwich
(D) One of Curly's dogs

29. The trademark poking in the eyes routine originated when?
(A) Curly was eyeing some starlets during rehearsal
(B) Shemp switched an empty can of beer for Moe's full one
(C) Larry tried to bluff Shemp in a card game
(D) Moe's older brother Irving lost his temper

30. In the beginning of Moe's career, Moe's mother, Jennie, was
vehemently against him teaming up with comic star Ted Healy.
What changed her mind?
(A) Two dozen roses
(B) Healy's offer to put a new roof on her house
(C) A performance from Ted, Moe and Shemp in her kitchen
(D) $100 for her synagogue building fund

31. The Stooges worked magic on the stage. Which Stooge's wife was
cousin to Harry Houdini?
(A) Moe
(B) Curly
(C) Larry
(D) Shemp

32. Even though Moe was unofficially the group leader, this Stooge actually earned more than Moe at one time?

(A) Curly-Joe
(B) Curly
(C) Larry
(D) Shemp
(E) Never happened, Moe was the 'Boss.'

33. By the late 1930s, it was clear to Columbia Pictures that the Stooges were a sensation. The Stooges were paid $8,000 per short, and were required to make eight shorts per year. How much were the Stooges paid for each short 20 years later?

(A) $25,000
(B) $50,000
(C) $70,000
(D) Never changed, it stayed at $8,000

34. Moe was a victim of an explosion in his home. What caused the explosion?

(A) A gas furnace
(B) A stove
(C) A barrel of wine
(D) A souvenir grenade

35. Throwing pies was another trademark gag of the Stooges. Who was considered the best shot?

(A) Moe
(B) Curly
(C) Larry
(D) Shemp
(E) Joe

Answers To A.A.M. Entrance Exam

How to score you're A.A.M. Local 6 7/8 Entrance Exam:

For every correct answer give yourself three points. For every incorrect answer give yourself a big fat zero. Add your total then divide it by 7/8 (for you math morons, you can multiply your total by .875).

1. (A) A labor union that provides protection for pie throwing. From the film *Half-Wits' Holiday*.   Score:_____

2. (C) $100. Tired of Ted Healy's shenanigans and unhappy with their pay and their role of being Healy's comic relief, Moe, Larry and Curly split from Healy in 1934.   Score:_____

3. (C) Jennie Horwitz was a successful real estate agent.   Score:_____

4. (C) Larry. Moe, Shemp and Curly were brothers (Horwitz), who later changed their name to Howard. Larry was not related.   Score:_____

5. (A) 190 shorts, 6 features.   Score:_____

6. (C) Under the name of The Three Stooges, their films were produced from 1934-1965.   Score:_____

7. (C) Four – Shemp, Curly, Joe Besser and Curly-Joe DeRita. Score:_____

8. (D) Three Stooges shorts with (C) a close second.   Score:_____

9. (D) Shemp. He was born in 1895, Moe in 1897, Larry in 1902, Curly in 1903, Joe in 1907 and Curly-Joe in 1909.   Score:_____

10. (E) A, B & C. These multi-talented actors also received training from the Wide-Awake Detective School. They were the top detectives at the Hyden Zeke Detective Agency.   Score:_____

11. (D) Major Hyde. As in Duck, Dodge and Hyde.   Score:_____

12. (E) The plucking of ukulele strings was used for this sound effect.   Score:_____

13. (A) Yiddish. The Stooges worked some of their Jewish heritage into their films.   Score:_____

14. (B) Curly   Score:_____

15. (A) Moe   Score:_____

16. (A) Moe   Score:_____

17. (C) Larry   Score:_____

18. (A) Moe   Score:_____

19. (C) Larry   Score:_____

20. (B) Curly   Score:_____

21. (C) They didn't marry sisters, but they would do just about anything for a laugh. Once Moe grew a beard only on the right side of his face, while Shemp grew a beard only on the left side of his face. During this period, they went to pick their visiting mother up at the train station. At first she didn't recognize them. When she did she was terribly embarrassed and said, "How can you do such crazy things? The people will think you're meshuga" (Jewish word meaning crazy).   Score:_____

22. (A) Moe sold frogs for 15 cents apiece or 10 for a dollar. For every dollar he earned, he would give his mother 70 cents. The other 30 cents was used for the theater. A dime for train fare, a dime for lunch and a dime to sit in the upper gallery. Moe would pick out one actor and study him intensely. He estimates that he saw from 60 to 70 dramatic plays between the ages of 11 and 13.   Score:_____

23. (D) Had Moe do it. Curly tried to open it but bent the tines on his fork. Moe, taking the fork from Curly, dropped a napkin on the floor, then asked him to pick it up. When Curly bent over, Moe hit him over the head with the crab, breaking the shell into a pile of pieces. Curly then tasted the meat, and made a face. He threw the meat away and proceeded to eat the shell cutting up his mouth in the process.   Score:_____

L-R Joe Besser, Moe and Larry

24. (D) Lucille Ball. Lucy worked with the Stooges in this 1934 film, and said what she learned was how to duck. Score:_____

25. (B) *Three Little Beers*. It's must-see viewing for serious golfers trying to perfect their game. Score:_____

26. (D) All the above. In 1958, in Bakersfield, California, Moe warned a belligerent customer that if he kept it up, he might go from 32 teeth to zero. A warning that even a Picklebrain would be wise to take seriously. Score:_____

27. (A) They started showing Three Stooges shorts on television. Back in 1958, the Stooges were in a bit of a rut. Night clubs weren't their forte, their film career was over and vaudeville was dead. Then Columbia pictures, though not holding out too much hope for their success, decided to sell old Three Stooges shorts, at bargain-basement prices to television stations. Almost overnight the Stooges' popularity exploded. They became one of the hottest children's property available. Millions of kids, who had never seen the Stooges before, went bonkers over these wild and crazy characters. Soon the Stooges shorts became the number one children's TV series in the country, beating out Popeye cartoons. Offers then came in from everywhere to do fairs, shopping center promotions, movies, TV and so on. The feature films were a direct result of this "Stooge Mania." Score:_____

8. (B) Veronica was one of Shemp's hens. The chicken escaped to a neighbor's yard, and after chasing the bird for a couple of days, Shemp got Moe to finally capture her. The next morning Shemp went to the local butcher and traded 12 live hens for six dead pullets. He held Veronica until last and gave her a whack in the eye before handing her over to the butcher.   Score:_____

9. (C) Larry tried to bluff Shemp in a card game. In a fit of rage, Shemp stood up, reached over and poked his fingers into Larry's eyes. Moe laughed so hard he fell backwards on his chair, crashing through a French door behind him. With his arm bleeding and tears coming out of Larry's eyes, Moe continued to laugh. From then on the rest of the world enjoyed this signature gag.   Score:_____

0. (D) $100 for her synagogue building fund. Jennie was a short woman slightly over five feet. According to Moe, she had incredible stamina, disciplined the kids and made all the decisions regarding the family without consulting anyone.   Score:_____

31. (A) Moe. He was married to his wife Helen for almost 50 years. She died six months after him on Oct. 31, 1975.

Score:_____

32. (D) Shemp. At the time the Stooges were being threatened by their old partner Ted Healy. Shemp was so scared he wanted to quit. To keep him on, Moe offered him 36 percent of the team's salary. Moe and Larry each received 32 percent.

Score:_____

33. (D) Never changed. Despite the fact that the Stooges were earning millions for Columbia, they never received an increase in pay. Columbia claimed the short subjects unit was not earning its keep. Fearful of losing the contract, Moe reluctantly never asked for a raise.

Score:_____

34. (C) A barrel of wine. According to Moe's daughter, Joan, Moe wasn't very careful when reading directions. When it was time to taste the wine, he pulled out the bung, and the entire contents of the barrel – wine, skins and seeds – exploded like they were shot out of a cannon. The white walls of the room were splashed vivid red. Moe was soaked with red wine, and was peppered with grape seeds from head to toe.

Score:_____

5. (A) Moe was a marksman. In the short *Slippery Silks*, Moe said he had a sore arm and face from over 150 pies that were thrown. In another incident, Moe asked and received a piece of blueberry pie from some dancing girls. He climbed to the top of the theater roof and let it drop on Larry's head for a bull's-eye. Racing up the building Larry ran into Moe and said, "Okay, dead shot, how come the blue on your hand matches the blue on my head?" Moe said, "I couldn't help it, Larry; I saw your head shining up at me and since it made such a nice target, I just couldn't resist testing my marksmanship."   Score:_____

TOTAL:_____

A.A.M. Entrance Exam Score

Add your total then divide it by 7/8
(For you math morons, you can multiply your total by .875)

TOTAL SCORE:

Grading Curve

73.50 to 91.87
Sorry, no brain-soygens admitted!

64.31 to 73.49
Hmmm… a fairly intelligent imbecile, there may be hope.

52.5 to 64.30
It's a no-brainer, you are eligible for the A.A.M. M.I.T.
(Morons In Training) Program.

52.4 and below
Congratulations, you are a true Moron!
Welcome to the A.A.M. Local 6 7/8.

This test was compiled, compelled and commingled by the prestigiou
accounting firm of Dewey, Cheatem and Howe. Candidates that failed t
qualify may still join by filing an affidavit that states under penalty o
perjury that the candidate is a *half-brother to a weasel*. Please send
notarized affidavit along with a note from a veterinarian to the A.A.M. car
of the Law Firm of Howard, Fine and Howard, Glendale, California, 91203

Amalgamated Association of Morons

On this _____ day of _____, in the year _____, by order of Chief Morons of the A.A.M. and the National Counsel of Morons representing A.A.M. Local chapters, hereby, thereby and whereby certify that:

Is a member in good standing of the Amalgamated Association of Morons, Local **6 7/8**. The above named inductee has achieved the status of:

☐ **True Moron**　　☐ **M.I.T** *(Moron In Training)*

Membership in this exclusive Association provides the above named to union protection for Pie Throwing, in addition and not limited to, entitling the member to unlimited Mulligans while engaged in the game of golf.

Duly signed and sealed by:

Howard, Fine & Howard

Howard, Fine & Howard　　Chief Morons, A.A.M.

MAKERS OF... FUN STUFF

AMALGAMATED ASSOCIATION OF MORONS
A.A.M.
Local 6 7/8
NYUK NYUK NYUK!

THE THREE STOOGES™ PHOTO *Album*

Moe was the second youngest of
five boys in the Horwitz family.

Shemp enjoyed a successful acting career on his
own and as a member of The Three Stooges.

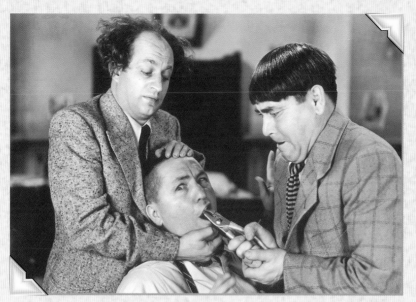

Hold still or I'll pull your gizzard out!

Happy trails.

Ready… aim… How about some fire boys?

Hey, look here, Moe, a note from the IR and S.

A couple of dumbells and an airbag.

Oh no! An IRS agent has arrived.

A sight for sore eyes.

We know a good dummy when we see one.
You're gonna be a big star.

It's Showtime!

Ready… Action… Roll'em.

The Stooges on top of their game.

The big shots with some beauties.

He's the captain you Knucklehead,
not the chaplain!

The cover girls dressed to kill.

We're pleading the 4th, 5th, 6th, 7th & 8th.

Shave and a haircut – two bits.

Heads of their class.

Perched partridge on a pickle brain.

And the beat goes on...

Woob... Woob... Woob...

Bubble trouble.

It's just about Slappy Hour.

This way for a Tunis fish sandwich.

What goes around comes around.

Face it, you're just a big baboon.

I want my mummy!

I don't see any loose wires up here!

Mind over manners.

We guarantee it!

He winked!

Roll'em right here boys.

Anybody home?

Prunin' a puddin' head.

The good, the bad and the chubby.

L-R Larry, Moe and Curley-Joe

First a banana and then a Havana–
you boys are good.

Hook, line and sinker,
fresh fish and a couple of stinkers.

SMASHING

GIFT IDEAS

- The Holiday Season
- "Boithdays"
- Golf Enthusiasts
- Business Gifts
- Father's Day Chuckles
- Three Stooges™ Enthusiasts
- Get Well Gifts (Hospitals), etc.
- Business Promotions
- Prizes for Golf Tournaments

From These
Legendary Comics!

Since 1929, The Three Stooges™ style of humor has been enjoyed by millions. With golf and The Three Stooges™ popularity at an all-time high, these novel gift ideas would be a welcomed addition to any Golf'n Stooges™ collection.

Bring Humor To The Tee-Box With Larry, Moe & Curly!

The Three Stooges™ Talking Golf Head Covers

Yes… they talk! Each character says two unique wisecracks to provide the poifect comment to your golf partners' less than perfect tee shot – a total of six unique one-liners recorded by the world's best impersonators. Simply squeeze the left hand and let them do the talking for you… "Nice shot Knucklehead™". They fit easily, even on oversized club heads!

Keep your Knuckles dry... Knucklehead™!

"Property of Three Stooges™ Country Club" Golf Towel. This towel is of exceptional quality with vivid colors and detail. Made of 100% cotton velour measuring 16"x 24" (large enough to polish Curly's baldhead). Golf towels are available separately or as part of a gift set.

Three Stooges™ Country Club Bag / Luggage Tag

Identify your golf bag or luggage with this prestigious Three Stooges™ Country Club Bag Tag. This tag clearly identifies the owner as a member of this exclusive Country Club and an official Golf'n Stooge™.

Country Club Divot Tool

Designed to repair Stooge™ size divots, after all, they were the experts when it came to divots! This heavy metal tool is engraved and embossed with the Country Club logo featuring a quality antique finish.

It's A Gimme

The Three Stooges™ golf gift ideas would make excellent gifts for the Golf'n Stooge™ in your life.

Accessories Fore The Golf'n Stooge™

The Country Club Accessory Set includes:

- ## The Golf Towel
- ## Bag Tag
- ## Divot Tool
- ## Six Golf Tees
- ## Deck of The Three Stooges™ Playing Cards

*Packaged together
in an attractive gift box*

Golf'n Stooge Desk Set

Golf... it Soitenly Beats Woiking!

Now, your woik day will be three times as fun with Moe, Larry and Curly by your side. These Golf'n Stooges™ will soitenly create a stir in any woikplace, and they're bound to put a smile on anyone's face... "Hey, Moe... I think Larry's got your ball!"

**Pens, Pencils &
Business Cards
Not Included.**

- **Hand painted and sculpted lightweight resin**
- **Holds and displays business cards, pens and pencils**
- **Each character stands approximately 4" high**
- **Desk set measures 10.5"w x 5.5"d x 5"h**

Official Country Club Time Pieces From the Greatest Knuckleheads™ of All Time!

Hey Knucklehead™…
It's time for a new clock!

The official timepieces from The Three Stooges™ Country Club Collection are available in two unique styles: The Three Stooges™ Country Club logo clock and the Greatest Knuckleheads™ of All Time! clock. These 11-inch wall clocks are constructed of high grade materials with a glass face and long lasting clock movement. Each clock is individually packed in an official Three Stooges™ Country Club gift box.

The Three Stooges™
Country Club clock

These are the chronometers of choice FORE the real Golf'n Stooges™

(requires 1 "AA" battery)

Greatest Knuckleheads™
of All Time! clock.

Hang'n With The Stooges

Your Knucklehead friends will love these key chains based upon The Three Stooges™ golf cartoon characters. These "Masters of Mishaps" have arrived in the form of PVC action figure key chains.

By combining the popularity of key chains with these little Stooges™, they're sure to produce big laughs.

- **Molded 3D characters**
- **Hand painted in vibrant colors**
- **Lobster claw and split ring for easy attachment to bags and backpacks**

Three Stooges™ Playing Card Gift Sets

This classic and decorative tin comes with **two decks** of Three Stooges™ Golf Cartoon Playing Cards. Each deck consists of 52 different hilarious golf cards in full color.

N'yuk, N'yuk, N'yuk.

It's for Soiten!

When playing with these enjoyable cards, card games have **never** been more fun.

Numbered Limited Edition Tin From The Three Stooges™ Country Club

A Certificate of Authenticity is included in each tin.

This limited edition tin is adorned and embossed with The Three Stooges™ Country Club logo on the cover. Affixed to the underside of the lid is a label identifying the tin as "Property of The Three Stooges™ Country Club" along with the tin's serial number. The tin also includes two decks of The Three Stooges™ Playing Cards, along with a fun and informational Three Stooges™ Trivia Book. One trivia section includes an entrance exam to join the prestigious *A.A.M. (Amalgamated Association of Morons) Local 6 7/8*. This exam will quickly determine if you're a "Wise Guy" or a "True Moron." ***Good Luck!***

Golf Tournament Prize Offer

Lighten up your golf tournament by giving the Three Stooges™ Golf Gift Sets as prizes for: Longest putt, closest to the pin (par 3's), farthest drive, worst drive, worst score or even host your own Three Stooges™ golf tournament. These gifts are fun, they're useful and they're poifect!

Also available, The Three Stooges™ Country Club Golf Playing Cards, featuring 52 different and hilarious golf cartoons in full color. It's the perfect complimentary entry gift for tournament players and volunteers.

Back of Card

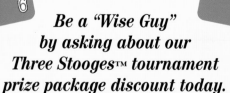

Be a "Wise Guy"
by asking about our
Three Stooges™ tournament
prize package discount today.

More Great
Gift Ideas

From

PaR™ SURVIVAL KIT
KEEPS YOU UP TO PAR!

- **Insulated Cooler with Durable 1-Liter Water Bottle**
- **Secret Pocket Inside Cooler – Hides Money or Credit Cards**
- **Cigar Pocket**
- **Lighter Holder**
- **Removable Shoulder Strap and Belt Loop**
- **Mesh Pocket for Score Card or Gloves**

Because golf is a game of skill, concentration and etiquette, organize your golf game with our uniquely designed insulated nylon pouch that's comfortable and convenient. Pockets and elastic straps hold all of your golfing essentials! Easily attaches to any golf bag, belt loop or simply sling it over your shoulder and you're on your way.

Because golf is a game of "Survival of the Fittest."

- **Pocket with Zipper**
- **Pencil Pocket**
- **Golf Bag Clip**
- **Divot Tool Pocket**
- **Tee Holders**

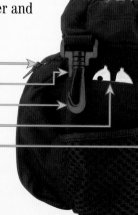

Another Fine Pair of Talking Golf Head Covers

Tee off with Laurel & Hardy™ in your golf bag and they will poke fun at your partners' less than perfect tee shots!

- Stan Laurel says 3 unique wisecracks and plays the Laurel & Hardy™ theme song. Oliver Hardy says 4 unique wisecracks. A total of 8 in all.

- Simply squeeze the left hand of the character to make it talk.

- These novel head covers are manufactured out of molded PVC with plush-style bodies and a knitted sock.

- The compact voice box is removable from its pouch located on the back of the head cover.

- Placing the golf head cover on the golf club is effortless due to an improved design that even fits oversized club heads.

- Requires only 2 "AA" batteries each.

167

MAKERS OF FUN STUFF

Gazelle, Incorporated
40940 County Center Drive
Temecula, California 92590

Phone: 888-442-0355 • Fax: 909-676-4199
www.golfinstuff.com • E-Mail: golfguys@golfinstuff.com

For additional Three Stooges™ products visit:
goknuckleheads.com